Previous Books by Calvin Bedient

Books of Criticism

Architects of the Self: George Eliot, D. H. Lawrence, and E. M. Forster
(University of California Press, 1972)

Eight Contemporary Poets
(Oxford University Press, 1974)

In the Heart's Last Kingdom: Robert Penn Warren's Major Poetry
(Harvard University Press, 1984)

He Do the Police in Different Voices: The Waste Land and its Protagonist
(University of Chicago Press, 1987)

The Yeats Brothers and Modernism's Love of Motion
(University of Notre Dame Press, 2008)

Poetry Collections

Candy Necklace
(Wesleyan University Press, 1997)

The Violence of the Morning
(University of Georgia Press, 2002)

Days of Unwilling
(Saturnalia Books, 2008)

THE
MULTIPLE

THE MULTIPLE

Calvin Bedient

OMNIDAWN PUBLISHING
RICHMOND, CALIFORNIA
2012

Cover Art by David Goldes
Pouring, 1994
Gelatin Silver Print
© David Goldes, Courtesy of the Artist and Yossi Milo Gallery, New York

green
press
INITIATIVE

Omnidawn Publishing is committed to preserving ancient
forests and natural resources. We elected to print this title on
30% postconsumer recycled paper, processed chlorine-free. As
a result, for this printing, we have saved:

2 Trees (40' tall and 6-8" diameter)
947 Gallons of Wastewater
1 million BTUs of Total Energy
60 Pounds of Solid Waste
210 Pounds of Greenhouse Gases

Omnidawn Publishing made this paper choice because our
printer, Thomson-Shore, Inc., is a member of Green Press
Initiative, a nonprofit program dedicated to supporting authors,
publishers, and suppliers in their efforts to reduce their use of
fiber obtained from endangered forests.

For more information, visit www.greenpressinitiative.org

Environmental impact estimates were made using the Environmental Defense
Paper Calculator. For more information visit: www.edf.org/papercalculator

Library of Congress Catalog-in-Publication Data

Bedient, Calvin.
  The multiple / Calvin Bedient.
    p. cm.
  ISBN 978-1-890650-66-7 (pbk. : alk. paper)
  I. Title.
  PS3552.E314M85 2012
  811'.54--dc23

                          2012015365

Published by Omnidawn Publishing, Richmond, California
www.omnidawn.com   (510) 237-5472   (800) 792-4957
        10 9 8 7 6 5 4 3 2 1
        ISBN: 978-1-890650-66-7

Contents

I

II

III

"Multiplicities are reality itself. They do not presuppose unity of any kind, do not add up to a totality, and do not refer to a subject."
—Gilles Deleuze

"If the universe is not-one, the rhapsodic is the avenue to truth."
—Alain Badiou

part **I**

(The billows puff they cannot lift their veilings)

After Bronzino

Who is this person does not take pleasure
in the things this thing does? Who does not
wish to have himself slapped like an egg
in a mantle in a wind in a hell of a tough

night? This thing come into my heart
many centuries old and cuss and sweat
and shake kiss migraine hurt and run,
a leaping ankle that thumb and trigger

finger adorn. Secretary of the six
female groans, this thing isn't smoke
of dogma this thing hasn't spoken for days,
this thing this thing this thing this thing.

propagation of the elements

Submit to the horror of sensible images?
A particle puts its groin to your mouth; go on,
make it swell in the garish heat of the marriage bed.
Incontinently you melt the glass Caesars.

Would you hold *another* down and make it eject
another? Another and another creep in this errant
trajectory.

    The orange clouds of evening are the nubs on my duvet.

EVENING IN THE COMPANY
OF UNDECIDED BIRDS

1

we are suspect men birds earth   wrists cuffed
   bent over the hood of evening

what are they asking what have we done?

who can blame the birds (whose hearts are a thousand chemicals)
that they hallucinate
the rayon day-cover of the moon?
who decides? who commands the visions of the beasts?

beloved be the mini-flashlights of their notes turned on too early fading
   now

birds too clover in the dusk to sing
hardly being *with*
neglected slight-wings of the ardent mother of atrocity

birds! she uses two eggs
cracks them in the middle

2

would you be the most violet beast listening at the wall
of the lectisterium   your shallow leek feet
curling on the sienna mesa of Melancholia?
are you leaf

15

men rustling in the little republic of breath?

can you oratory a little queen to say I love you at the vanity table of
    everything?
or take a seat yourself before the absent mirror?
there, do you see yourself
Ariel in tights striped spook applying a foundation?

what is that look when you pause   just a look?
not bitter in essence as Dido is bitter?
do you too like it black
waved like a limp licorice wand before an orchestra of terror?

eat the scream in your mouth no one will know you ate it,
you punk you dodger of rains children still fling themselves into

3

the huffing accordion commotion of Becoming's a broken idea
there is a boiling-together rather an El Greco thigh
or three condors fighting over an elephant
folio or the vapor-choked station of St. Lazare
blotting its sentences at this darting juncture

                        a watch clouded by breath

ah, if the senses could burst the multiplication table
freakishly all-tissued and the concept accept its femme

or would it be heaven just to be AMONG
the least exposed AMONG the most exposed
muffled in an antiquity without period

fields and fields of atoms not saying anything not blowing?

the evening big and small

knows it is to all
that each is called
as one who would be called
hyaline

the rain in the roof of the mouth not zenithal get down and on foot
find your hat or not you are the rain's
silverheaded cane   a luxury

the rain tapping at matter's root as at a wonder

RAPID DOLLY

monday,
tiny
lightning
bolt
on the
edge
of—

darkened
pronouns'
rain
on the
wind's reels

congratulations, birds that sleep all night
without once falling out of the trees

(how strange sleeping things are among the leaves)

Deception Falls

O doctors of the falls, there was a cleaning establishment here, it tried
       on my father's gray suit, my mother's blue dress, forgive
       its presumption, it wanted to know their animal reserve,
       reverse diorama of their silences, of which I was the
       uproar, fleeing

O doctors of the spits, the "I" was a plunge pool where, now here, now
       there, a dead distempered puppy leapt as if to catch a ball,
       and a woman with rainbow trout locks pounded the keys
       of a rocking upright and sang, "Cuddle up and huddle up
       with all your might. Oh, Oh" while a man on the slippery
       bank cranked the cold engine of the snow

O doctors of the city, it was on East Sprague that you taught my
       brother to play the violin, until he was a high E note
       walking around the house blindly with distemper while I
       fingered the bitch nipples of a clarinet and mother played
       the whip saw she had anchored in father's fly, once upon
       we were living in the vacuum tubes of krauts and allies

O doctors of the ringworm, your two nylon-capped flappers, rather
       pretty boys, escaped on the horns of the Great Northern
       railroad, were recaptured, always new in town holding
       back each other's spilling brotherly bowels

O doctors of the rebuff, not in the history of butterscotch corduroys
       nor in the cysts on the bicycle's forehead nor in the roller
       skate key's mislaid mouth did you plant your image but
       in the comet of the sock you distributed the semen of the
       dead while high in the forests virgins rode bareback the
       wet black bark of the bears

O doctors of the butcher-shop, the finger-painting on your aprons is
        the masterpiece in my chest, I ignore it, I am salty like
        a cloud, clean like a vertical, watery like an onion, tasty
        like a fishtail. The hundred cries of Deception Falls pour
        through my veins, the pangs so cold it thrills, I will not
        go back to the plaid shirts of the catalogues, the epileptic
        popcorn dark of shrill matinées, father's pocket watch shut
        up like a leaky secret in his pocket

O doctors of the archeologies, who jerk off to valedictions, goodbye,
        goodbye, I say fie to everything that doesn't hurt so much
        as always, much always, and for so long. Those who have
        been too little born, and too much, shake themselves
        like a cat in a dog's mouth. Yet in the urgently swollen
        hurt hours they escape into a monstrous delusion, as of
        a heavy orange popsicle-slushy burning *struggling* moon
        rising from the dead smell of practice rooms, and play
        themselves *out there* like a guitar of tigers snarling in the
        "in" existence

O doctors of industrial strength, bring me an acetone high, for I
        would bang sharp at the window of the spike while
        feeling Up caffeinated hair with airplane ride on it
        whirring through the quantum flocks' drunken lurches at
        inexistence

O doctors of smudges, burning sage to purify the spaces, the measure
        of the age is enormity not the enormous, the moons
        have been routed from their papery nest, they cannot
        find the bowels / of the rose, they are angry,   they are
        meateaters now, the bastards

Yes, doctors of the falls, bald-faced hornets sing in the splintering
        piano; yes, doctors of the butcher-shop, bloody wasps
        swarm your display cases; yes, doctors of the city, the
        musicians are playing the backs of the yellow jackets, the
        bright stripes and the dark

Virility Wrapped in an Army Blanket by a campfire under the Bridge in Winthrop, Washington

It was there that a headless chicken ran, excited with news,
while your father stood unmanned in the yard
holding the short red skirt of the ax.

War, a Problem

Will technology kill the brotherhood of war? Probably. It is a problem.

Is brotherhood itself a problem? A love so strong it compels you to go back and get shot at with your brothers?

Oh the beauty of brotherhood so sweet so painful

You cannot sing it it is heavenandhell

It makes fighting in a war a sacred thing though the war itself be evil

Inside is the sacred outside is the killing

Do you see that there is a problem here?

Bonding is a weapon and sacred

Do you deny that war guarantees this experience?

Do you deplore it?

You aren't heartless are you?

stud whiskers

Some men are like the bees
they want a destruction

    Without self-transformation
the historical male decays,
        so difficult now, mother,
in these Capitalism will eat you days

Like bees that crawl on an egg hot from the hen's ass
        (they do not know *what's* inside
        they will kill this thing hot from the hen's ass),
they're toxic, with just a little delicacy
in the sensory department

Area 51, Groom Lake, composition by field—
is that what you want, to spread the radiation around?

The soul sits up looks about like a rabbit
expecting probably a thing of youthful blood

but the west is old

Belief, we gave you all our heart, didn't we, daddy?

        What
        could have
        gone wrong?

Look, the mother is walking aside
in what I call "transcendental ontology,"

        the "tall" part   sticking its   head up
        over the trench (well, you cannot say I have not warned her)

If she were Marx's mother, would she be sorry?
Even Venus could not be so sorry

Where have all the revolutions gone?
Invisible hooks pull at the poets' mouths
Is there a new art? You wander the desert,
     looking for the new art

Who now will hum the undollared basis of all comparisons?
The imagination isn't capitalist, you know,
     it rabbits in phenomenalistic little hops —

          a pretty

                    move
          easy to pick off

          (oh be cured of that)

Back in Area 51
the F-117
Nighthawk
Ø nicknamed
Harvey after
Harvey the rabbit
Ø got down
into the hole
and exploded the
fucker wrote up
the paperwork
we need to take out more
targets on a single sortie

"I CAME OUT OF HABITATIONS WHERE WARMTH FILLED MY FEET AND LOINS"
—ROUSSEAU

living in actual ass under the stars Josie's experiment

easy access to parking and bushes

the first few times I feel awful flattened myself against the wall

easy access to bulk movements of air

dear souls "open themselves up, enraptured, to the essence of all things"

marshmallow chimes blown on by a flamey wind

we're made of the same stuff you and I matches benzene drop zones

you see this wound in my thigh a brief history of Vietfly

I say screw the bag lady who called me prince and said I did nothing for
    my people

what does a spider feel in moonlight?

marriage riding its dark horse

a child I tried to climb the black cast iron vine of my mother's sewing
    machine to learn how to sing at the school of the silver wheel but
    thread-chatter got in the way bunch-talk the needle stabbed mama's
    finger good we called it off

pagoda of dirty dishes in the sink she threatens to kill me she's upset

I say the sea is a warning full and prompt

the wave-shovels cannot pick up the dead duck fucking waves hats off
    to the dead duck

how many reels exhaust the image history of the person

it would be lovely to heal in a little muck called never mind

multitude

Of one hand painting the Sistine Chapel ceiling, multitude;

of people hiding behind doors, multitude;

of cloudlets soft as foreskin, multitude;

who can avoid it who can bear it, multitude.

Rubbing The Hairs on The Back of a Man's Thigh

The woman in me stands at the door watching for her man
        to fly down from the sky.
"Jesus, get a move on." She wants me to be
three, four, six, eight times
more trumpeting than the elephant rains.

Galoshes in the snow are not dearer than the man in me
when the woman in me
is weeping and bedewing herself
like a sloppy lot of dew.

"Do right by me," she says,
"Get good reviews, astonish
foolish distractions
with your smell of the whole"

(has collapsed
is discouraged already).

"Dead," her eyes say. "You'll have sex with a tomb."

I hate her eyes her eyes have come
sleepless out of the bedroom of the crystal.

There are as many universes as there are phrases

You, you, would you
let time be
empty of us? Bring on
your verbal floats

covered with wet roads
knolls first kills . . .
parade the collapsing
universes of your phrases;

life only *is*
because there's a void
to despise. I can't

stop to explain this to you
I am playing in the
lusciously worlded up
dirt in the yard, grinding
my yellow truck up the shovel-

patted road, shuddering
like my father in his bull
dozer not that we like him
he snores on the couch
sneaks out to bars pinches
one nostril to blow
snot out the other
shoots rabbits in his wild-

smelling coat. I'll say this,

he should have told her he
loved her and just once
he could have called me *pal*
like the father who
helped his little boy
pee in the john today

—oh such a universe
all at once
engulfing my face.

Screw his home from
work don't bother me
grunts anyway we
we don't have to say
don't touch me today
I don't want your death
to annoy me he knows.

You men, stingy with
your phrases
when the women
are about, using
death to get back at life,
that woman, you
rub your behind in it,
a dog dragging its ass

across the grass.

You shouldn't have
made her crazy you should
left her dress
weighted with the
feathers of tomorrow.

What's molested is lost
in three voids, the not-
identical-with-itself,
the if I'm a beast
where's my beasthood,
the echo void of
amazons crying.

I can't stop to explain
every little thing
to you, I no longer
write about the personal,
my theme is the moment
—bottomless, self-
destroying—and anyway

the door of the trailer has
opened she steps down
like a long-legged bird
testing a thawing river,

watches me play,
smiles, turns away.

Quick I must find a
phrase for her come back
I have a phrase for you
*the men hurt the women
unspeakably* wait I can think
of a better one *the women
hurt the men unspeakably*
no I can't do this
I am death.

If I had a cluster of
universes to hang
at her ears (red Bakelite,
ticky, a white satin blouse,
she must be off
to a dance) why, you ask,
would she listen
to a single one (ah, reader,
you are so on top of things
you must be death)
if my theme is the
Adams of a more
terrible Eden
and the Eves?—

and so I say in all

uselessness and grief,

The sky-bell didn't see
the sheeny sweep
of the doll's blond hair

in the rear
window of a car on I-
40,

its head
dead as cast-off
undies. Stars

fell like buckshot
on the antelope
slopes.

I was a foot-pedal of
the night I-
40. I heard
the sand

paradise
complain
of naked ladies.

The Mojave doesn't ring
even a single grain
disdainful
of water caresses.

You laugh
like someone
who found childhood
charming. The head

bell flicks the next
date up
in its calendar of tears.

The Gordon Stewart Northcott Murders of Boys in Wineville, California, 1928

The bodies of boys are delicious to torment

You keep them in a rickety chicken coop in the dark

You visit them there your nephew Sanford Clark visits them there laths of sunlight lashing their faces

You feed them twice a day like chickens

After using them you cut them up sprinkle lime bury the parts

You regularly fuck Sanford Clark he's old fifteen but he's family

He helps you kill the throwaway boys

One day he'll tell on you

His sister Jessie came down from Canada to fetch him she tried to kill you three times she's no good at killing

Gordon Stewart Northcott once decapitated a nameless Mexican boy

Americans have killed a lot of Mexicans

It is regular to kill if you are an American

Canadians too are sometimes killing

Sarah Louise Northcott a Canadian mother said she killed Walter Collins son of Christine Collins an American mother

Sarah Louise Northcott said her own son was her daughter's son

She said Gordon's father was his father

She said Gordon had been fucked by every member of the family

Arthur Hutchins Jr. of Illinois said he was Walter Collins of California

Arthur Hutchins Jr. had run away from his stepmother she did not want him she was an unpleasant person

He was caught in DeKalb and asked if he was Walter Collins

A drifter at a roadhouse had told him he looked like the Walter Collins had his picture in the paper

The authorities wanted him to be Walter Collins he said yes that's me I am Walter Collins

Christine Collins said this boy is not my Walter the Los Angeles police said how can that be take him home for a couple of weeks you will see

The L.A. police were needing to look good photographers were there it was an occasion

Walter Collins's little dog knew Arthur J. Hutchins, Jr. to be Walter Collins and his cat knew it too and his friends knew it also but Christine Collins did not know it

After two weeks Christine Collins went back to the police she said the dental records do not agree that this Walter Collins is my Walter Collins

She was put in a mental institution for not recognizing her own son

Code 12 means you are a difficult person Christine Collins was code 12

We have enough troubles already said Captain Jones of the all-the-time-looking-bad L.A. Police Department

Reverend Gustav Briegleb of Pasadena schemed to get Christine Collins out of the looney bin

Gustav Briegleb was a German the good German

But Arthur Hutchins Jr. confessed I lied I wanted to go to California to see Tom Mix the police had to release Christine Collins

She was nobody then and Arthur sold junk at carnivals he was nobody then then he became a jockey he had an exciting life

But Gordon

Gordon Stewart Northcott was a Canadian we do not want him in our country

Said "Believe me, officers, that chicken ranch was a butcher shop"

Said to the court "oh the mental torture of killing children you would not know"

There is an urge to kill an object against which one has an objection

Is man just weak?

Man is weak and woman is weak

Besides there is no thunder in boys' slender bodies they are easy to kill

They are Halflings not even sexual except in a someday sort of way

How frightened they look they do not know what is happening to them

They are you Gordon Stewart Northcott you must kill them

Are we agreed that we understand Gordon Stewart Northcott?

He had a really shoddy mind you could not find anywhere a shoddier mind

Well his mother had a shoddier mind it wasn't even there

She confessed to all the murders like a regular noble mother but she was irregular

35

Gordon's father was stupid not to know what was going on at the ranch

Likely he was lying which is shoddy shoddier still not to tell the police family loyalty yada besides he was probably his son's grandfather I can't tell you how shoddy that is

Captain Jones of the Los Angeles police department was all in a day's work shoddy

When Gordon Stewart Northcott came athwart them Lewis and Nelson Winslow had run away from home to pick cantaloupes in the Imperial Valley

Lewis was 12 Nelson 10 such stupid little boys

Gordon Stewart Northcott asked Lewis and Nelson Winslow to accompany him to his chicken ranch in Wineville

You must be very careful in America

You must not run away from the people who hate you

You must not leave your yard if you are a scrumptious little boy

You must not come into the country if you are a Mexican

You must not cross the L.A. police they have Code 12

You must not go anywhere near Wineville California it is too ashamed to exist anymore

You must not have an ax in your shed

You must not have an ax in your hand

You must not let the rest of your family fuck you

There must not be anyone else in your family

36

Family are all very dangerous

You must not defend yourself in court poor soul you claim it is your right you are just not clever enough you are boring but you want to treat what you did as a fucking amazing story oh go ahead make a fool of yourself

You must not live on a remote farm with other crazy people

You must not pretend to raise chickens when you are really interested in something else

You must get out of the country

You must not go to Germany

As for the Mexicans they don't want you

The Mexicans never did want you

You are an impossible person

The Roses of Your Dementia

shout at the Notional Tree. Why should only they hang by the neck, red with exasperation?

From the twenty folds of childhood *broke into a musky sweat.* You sniff yourself: *this unhappy god this disguise of poison.*

The sacred quality of the multiple, is it still crawling in the mind, palpating things like the soft black hands of the boss bees on the snapdragons' abdomens?
Does it smell like green fire when you open the book of the trees?

You grow tall. Thripped. Provoked. Afraid to betray the huge potato in the tongue
       (your thung still rooted in the utherus)

Oh to flap like a flag in galactic wastes
               —nobody knowing it is there,
                          hee! hee!

It will be a cold day when the clockdusk
blows on its hands
before adding up an unfinished life.

Meanwhile, how much money you got? Give me some. Culture baron. Your legendary wealth.

Fewer are the hymns when you walk a mile or two below your first love.

Oh, miniscule, mortal visibility.

Nipples encircled with clauses

May calculates too much you have heard her
click her teeth with 1 2 3 4 polished tines
edgewise from Wednesday printing her eyelids
5 6 7 no my God 8 rough drafts with silencers

       Swimming from guano island to guano island
           it wasn't I who sang, "I'm not coming back"

          Nana in the sunset secretly trembling

          Cloudy handful secretly trembling

  The table where you shovel animal, padrone

O blue piano chili this bloodied cotton

Floating Ant

Wednesday | bares the turned
page of her shoulder | Thurs-
day's the feral | cat with the
swollen balls | Here they come |
the leaves riding in from Dead
Rock | unshaven | filthy | Are
these the townsfolk | selling
their dolls | woven on tongue
depressors? Oh to fly over
Cripple | Creek | dropping
leaflets of a leafy | color
all over town | Friday ducks
to Sunday | under the | red
blades of the Blackhawk sun.

Bridge of Hair

Socrates had his demon honk
if you have a demon

You have been rowing the
whole wet of your mouth

The imagination wants a
creatureliness all its own

There may be too much priapus
in snow's motion

The thunder plops its flesh-folds
in dirty baths

What a foot to suffer so little so
close to the earth

The wind "gives you its hand under
your clothes"

Can we just dispense with forms?

I feel it is not a fair question

I do not like you to ask it

I have nothing more to give just
angular face

Not on my piano

Why I am shouting what
universe leave?

Not ragging on my piano

Look to your crotch get out of
my wolf

Nijinsky's legs were a goat in a red
pepper meadow

In a red pepper meadow Nijinsky
was not just Diaghilev's meat

In bed with eternity I
discourage her pawings

He took the hooks out of the night
he was a ton of naked

Moon like deer lard

A reference groping the night

You wouldn't dare you wouldn't
dare

rays of the territory

1

The fruit my sister rain grew was two blue
leaves short of satisfaction the air was snatch

2

or slip, day a knight backing
across the board, balancing goose

3

berries on a table knife, the clouds
a '48 Chevy visor lowered against the sun.

4

Life was a skip rose nobody jumps in. So I ate
them things, heart, all those things

5

I had thought to call my little ones.

6

I was already in addition very dangerous
nervous-languaged irregular with a mother.

7

Who can be a hero
if he snows on his own breast
like the Russian tongue, until,
finding the loneliest things,
he showers *likes* on them,

8

light, feathery *likes*,
so as not to hurt them,

9

little satiny ribbons of cold?

10

I knew I could out
stray any house
organization, like yellowtails swishing around,

11

swishing around in a coral reef,
matches craving more and more summer.

12

A brute? I can show you *that*
sort of hero, the one who sings:
my people are the cicadas in Arcadia
you dare not touch
the electricity of our tree,

13

his sensibility a fender on which a buck
hangs its extinguished chandelier. Listen, Joan,

14

ignore the smell of unfresh clothing in
John's letters, the fat odor of a hunter's coat

15

hanging over the back of your chair
as you read them. You know he likes

16

your different smell, your *before the wars false acacia* smell
is how he would put it if he weren't

17

dressing the deer, tearing its envelope
to get at the meat. Even in
razoring cold

18

the hero is in love with day,
vicious day, our long fanatic.

part **II**

(the ear readies itself to hear meat living)

the breathing place

the man behind the (desk
couldn't find my report on you
meanwhile (I saw
your face on a T-shirt (thought:
you look a bit simple, (washed out
but (at the sound of your
living (adjunct to the (sky's
breath-vacancy (as if (such that
your lungs were opportunists,
ladder steps (barely there,
pursuits, drawings-in of
(tree (field (*is* (I scorn
the report (nor would
make of you, suspiring,
or of any (expiring,
a palmful of memory-pollen
(pasteurized (worked into
(honey's (second heaven—
(*especially* you, wilding
even now (the surface of
(living, suing for anything at all
(a bulb cell-
suing for anything at all
(lungs launched into too
much air —(not in you
the charm of Watteau's
"delicate musician"
holding her A
K-like (instrument
among the darkened leaves
(leaves in nobody's doll
(mimicking their
embellishments—you
(unschooled (bare-sprung
into the no thing/
everything of origin's
left-over (nows

47

(are they scalding?
(elixir? (here in the ripe
Alpha catastrophe of
light (its unmatchable
descriptive faculty
(what then now do you know
horripilating when things
come over you
all peculiar suddenly

THε OβSCURITY OF THε TεN DRεSSεS

night
       exposes the imposture of perspectives,

but immense day—

           isn't it fabulous, 'Annah?
come and meditate,

           your conviction is my sister,
              employing so many stratagems.

now to get down to the wind's pain, take it apart, see,

      it's gone,
      so many stratagems.
                    soeur harmonie, soeur passant.

the sound of the gathered crows
      rises like a burning thatch. the grief

   of being masculine and knowing it,
      the serpent soft to touch in the dust

   of the language,
           dry patches in the garden. glooms

lit like an airfield. nothing comes. and now the torch of your stride.

The foresters of the verse
hunt the Venus of numbers:

Season luce
arrives,

the partridges in the cedars
                              sleep irritated and green,
the sun scratches tulips out of the dirt,
                              "co-" makes sense,
                    "and" is a sovereign good.

How *now* the role habitual
that each accrues,
          terrace of clarity over the sad resemblances?

               (this is they; they cannot be seen,
                    they are too familiar).

The collar of strawberries
is the fur of my femme.

But, look, already Venus flees,
                    her back strafed with meters—

     lingering awhile, there where the cereals
     seethe with the dark angels of matter.

A STORM OF COMMAS WAS COMING

Heraclitus
on fire with Heraclitus
    /is lost in the rain again,
        /// slashes streamy, the way an oracle speaks.

During the season of commas,
                the minnows
do not contradict the current,
their standstillity
        is a trick,
           see,
they flick—

I love their springy motility,
        their slipperiness in the hands of the critique.

It is positively SPITTING commas,
      it's MARVELOUSLY commatic—

    all the commas, crossing the water like horses,
             (without a crossing
    is no Sierra).
        Tell me what is happening,
    where are you going, your pores so open?

Alas, bad things happen to commas, such as:
    they drag a limp leg, they pant,
        their sex hangs crooked,
their name means "piece cut off."
        This is horrible.

I have attended to their technical reflections
and tasted their hurrying-to-the-dumb-place tears.

WHOSE DAY?

My morrow died in (my (shotgun; my tongue when it (stepped
(mock-gingerly like a (hen secretly resigned
  to the shit it's in. *Hola*, whose day is this,

its new-washed khakis smothered in mother-dust?
Swing your machetes, angels, against our weedy
parts (show a little love. Here! keep back from the

inner organs, they're not lunchbox oranges
or a young girl's tits budding on the day, they
(and their worms (are hiding . . .

                Word is out!
Day has lost her Ovidian ovaries.
Quick, in what stone-carrying carts (on what
rocky roads (under what splatter-gas galaxies

(will you find them? Already they're on their
way, pickups loaded with solvents, prods, voice-
tackles, grafters hidden from those whose days

are different from ours, days (so they say (never
punk'd, whose *hi* has somebody in it, whose arm
(pits are washed by the jet stream, whose zeros

are frauds, whose love's not a (blonde whose child
is called *utterly* (*impossible*, whose screws
are not the ejecta of a mad machine.

Right here, under heavenly showpieces of dust,
the Black Eye, the Red Spider, the Bubble,
the Exclamation Mark, the Lost (whose days

are a gas hustle display (mocked at by dark
matter's (smoked glasses, you will find *our* day,
or call it whose day ("whose" as in "whose,"

52

there is no deception here, "day" as in—
but what I began to explain (and only
to you, my friends, (has to do with . . . might be termed

(the unexperienced: "un" as in alt-,
haloed in oddity, mystagogy
contrary to the Cartwheel, the Atom for Peace,

all that great trashy scatter overhead.
The soul in its recombinant function
 is what I mean, I mean working the room

of the dark, despite melancholy with its
(plate of doubt and (side of grief, whose days
are (slow Asias of time, their seconds jacked—days

whose table is quitted sooner than is polite
by the hombres of perfume and the fillies
of cigars (peppy folk whose day must have been

a hoot, for how they laughed and laughed (they conversed
like mules that stomp death into the ground. I
could almost wish them back again, swelling

the room like day amid the minutes (but
it was careless of them to caress once
or twice (the chef of my contagions, whose

meringue is the melancholy of my hands.

Turning aside from the vulgar to think

I wore the piano's baggy-assed pants
in a musical lurch of *buenos*
when others smiled, though
everything smelled ponk like Peru.

In reality I was
WET CHALK,
several, probably, WET
CHALKS swimming together,
our elbows carat-accents
in the glutspeak of the Hudson.

Having stubbed God out with thinking
I tried to burn down in my own springy flame,
god-like,
as Zarathustra preached to the groundlings.

Then I tortured out an analogy
such as never before had maddened the earth,
"lovelier, obscurer, extremer than anything."

Next I became a Conceptualist.

Good humored though we was
we was evicted summarily from the down
town Manhattan Holiday Inn
for our installation of jabbering plaster

      (stood for what it mean what it mean
      to coldcock
      the Renaissance studio idea)
      (pack it up you self-important gods
      was our motif).

West, then, to the Peacock Bar
in Spokane's Davenport Hotel,
having elected to be
elegantly historical.

But when a peacock hopped up and lazy
Susaned on our table,
we laughed to have such venereal plumes
sweeping our faces, tickled
at not being able to see
in the very behind of beauty.

Everything Suck Big Suck Big Six Buttons

The squid writing Cloud-Pump on the clouds
wait to fall down women's blouses.
They wriggle their roots above my 3-watt
nipples are their flashlights when the night is blue.
But I am through with bleating at the berrygates.
Paint a cherry if you want the milk of love.

A bare ash Venus scatters now my sack
of twigs. I have had it with material girls   everything
and boys, 73 rolling around on a bed,   suck
fat Uccello horses—they have *none* of the Qual-   big
ities, just swells, ouch, reddenings, "*love* that."   suck
They're poor like *that*. They love that.   big

Who will pet the tiger throws on industry
leader's knees? Upon whose airs will I rise,
a shimmering chord of exquisitivity
sharked from the meat-holes in the choir's faces,   Venus
females to the virile smell of burning money?   scatters
Snow that fell arrest early this marmalade.

Lean on me, moment, lubricate my organs.
Can I still spit on the red square and the blue?
Next to the tree frogs singing near the sky,
it's you I love, my Kilimanjaro pad,   milk
your Eden skin, your axis knees. And   of
after that the little sparrows of the fire.   love

I've climbed the dozen-fruit tree of the palette
and painted the wind wearing the sleet coat
of universal autobiography.
But for you, Mother Fish, I make my delicatest
drawings, in a boat floating over your cold
ardor where the bones have no harbor.

Here is a turquoise fly, still damp; take it;
and here a coral twig, a tiny hair of the sea.

"Schubert on the Water, Mozart in the Din of Birds"

—Mandelstam

The problem is the core, or lack of same,
a ghost must live here it's so cold.
Well, not "live."

And so, approaching the indefinite brink of you,
I can be anything, eyes that can't focus
absent instructions come apart
and the images barely reach you with their love
intact. For they do start from love, you know.
Did you think they were meant to be catastrophes?

For instance, zeppelins. You may see them as fat
floaty things flying low over your head,
but descend with me now
into the motor gondola. *Feel the vibrations.*
A purr—think of being inside a purr.

Such sights we could share!
L. A. at night,
the millions of delicate lights,
the geometry no one has filmed it's so large—

if it were projected on a screen
the corners wouldn't be visible,
we are nauseous there is too much world to show,
love in the parks.

SONATA, WHAT DO YOU WANT OF ME?"

—Fontenelle

Step into the boat for a watergive hurrying circumstance. Be seated.
Everything here is thicker and banger, as when (look!) in the blue tent
    you look lilac.
Yes, here you're good you're energetic. In the slipped-down sky you've
    water's practical humor.

The clumsy sculpture of a carriage unhorsed at an inn's
between laughing. Fetch the driver, take along a throw,
purple is best mohair softest saddest and four and four more bars
                for the occasional sea-cleft window aahs.

My slow part's a fragile mask thrown anyhow on the floor,
until window curtains make a silk bright swan,
              which is how they fly when opening.

After church music's tall stained glass you'll like me feather
and bug and oak and row, where a rapt surrounding water
floats the shadow of a stranger with a bracketed kindness.

Once I lift my hand to start there's a silence none can bind,
except to a fanatical point of accuracy, like a lightning bootlace.

In later years you'll startle when I treat you as a cabbage atrocity,
so low down is the mouth whose "human reek of blood"
smiles on me. Your whole family of hearing will want to burst into tears.

But for now I'm content to blow on the dead white powder of your manners
and to hear you say, "Never have I seen so much moonlight."

"MILLIONS OF STRANGE SHADOWS ON YOU TEND"
—Shakespeare, sonnet 53

what would be more agreeable, to be Jean whose blue eyes are a running
    stream over small [obstructions (until Jeanette lights the blue candles)
or Paul "breathlessly eager" to "enjoy her favorable comment," e.g.,

that his face in the late apple-juice light was almost too much beauty,
    like bark chopped off a cedar or a yellow bee
ticking clockwise on a red clover—not less choice

than that? (certainly she was pleased to be at dinner
    with one so breathlessly eager.) and regard Jeanette, who thinks
happiness a swaying *bridge* and *not unlike* (sit near her, Paul, she's

taken a liking to you). a flag on which I sew a sprinkler's mathematics
    tells how *much* can be locally disclosed of waters formerly infuriate.
what would be more agreeable, to be Jeanette's white neck pecked by Paul?

well, she wants Jean now, cold Jean—stupid Jeanette—
    whereas Paul—vain, drunk, *and* stupid—wants everyone.
reader, I know you miss the romantic master-pieces of yesteryear,

you're like thinking how can anything come to *be* now, distinct,
    like to an orange bee on a pink clover. yes, they all drum on "like,"
the likenesses, as if to hear the discriminate/indiscriminate rain.

SHEER

Not a one doesn't shrink from ontology,
not a one is not let down
by the peppering. Who hasn't
batted back leaves

and not missed a plain geometry,
a simple, tidy sum,
like the count of one for once
to keep off the fucking fury?

Like Animal in *Stalag 17*
had a thought of Betty Grable,
fell to the floor, why wasn't she with him,
bear though he was, the bore?

Anyone would want to be in one
of her nylons with her in it, too.
And is it true a nylon fills with air
when rubbed against a plaster wall?

Anyone would want to end there, then,
as that kind of one, a million
netted in the gorgeous vanity of style.

CHEETAH

"You take death to go to a star," van Gogh said,
he rode in a car of sunflowers,
he could not go very far.

How long our diaphaneity—
the inside inside out to the outside?
Are they enough, the lovely differences,
the round clouds' cheetah spots on the desert floor?

See how they gallop away from Dead Rock.

Who wants to be Miro's *nu a la baignoise,*
just blue in the blue, swimming la la secret
somewhere blue, swimming her own shadow blue,
blue cloud shadows on her somewhere blue,
blue wings closing blue on blue?

Better the umber nipples in a see-through blouse,
        a la Renoir,
the cheetah spots hunting on the tawny floor.

                            for MF

part

(if you were a nude with as many arms as a ladder)

WITNESS SAID HE SAW THE DEFENDANT BEAMING DEFENDANT WAS ALONE AT THE TIME

Witness when questioned said defendant left air and water where he
　　found them.
"I saw insects with legs like grass stems sequestered in his clothes," he said.
"A ballooning wood tick hung from each ear.
No, I wouldn't say he looked unhappy.
He had itty-bitty feet that tried to hold on to the underside of a
　　particularly hairy salmonberry.
After that I found him very often sleeping on my chest like wings,
　　which you know don't really look asleep they just look quiet.
When we reached dry grass he I don't know how to put it *fripped*
　　himself into a grasshopper.
They sound so angry but I fished with him for four or five hours and
　　he seemed charmed by the songs I hummed under six layers of Bud
　　Light breath.
Oh, no, I couldn't recall them now I was in a transport perhaps.
Fish? He spat them out.
You could be a wade he said lets ball up.
It sounded inappropriate.
I have a hundred like you he said waiting winking at me on the river
　　like the busty aluminum girls on an eighteen-wheeler's mud flaps.
I began to feel uncomfortable.
Coop, I said, coop coop coop coop.
There were eggs between my thoughts. I felt colored at the tips, a sort of
　　mustard plant on a sun day when you're chin-up to the cloud bar.
I was on my back when he went over me like an old boat.
I never saw him again until this afternoon.
Yes, that's him over there.
Ask him how we got married.
My wife sent a clipping.
Ask him do we have any chicks.
When I listen to him breathing at night I'm glad he's not there.
Something about him, a bit Mergansery, wet wet.
These flutterings were they tricked awake do I look like the sort of man
　　you can do that to?
What I have here is a tongue exactly scrabble. Wagtail. I could kink.

Whatever he did was extra and by cheep I'll have him plucked and
scatter all nestlings of the floating kind.
I'll have him barred and weathered. How perfect is that."

hiPPo, the logic of THIS MUSIC, To WALk ON THE BOTTOM OF SUCH coPiA

1.

Dear, you could be—more Viennese. Scatter-
baffle—as the wind—chings the trestle. The way

to shrink—a la Dulles—is to be: dull soldier
dull soldier dull. You are so many more

when there's a relaxation. The new hearing
mutes the analysand. Sand, tintinnab-

ulating sand—is what it likes, trickling.
"Now I understand you, everything can be

a lens. The winds will return clearer." Yes—
and dearer, with more *everywhere* than *here,*

no sickness in the package. The eyes enter the weather.

2.

The lost chord innumerable in the dark
hubbub of the stars—unscorable—is

nothing you'd want to hear—with the baby bye
bye shell of the ear, that flushed upside down

treble. You say, "the evening is a wolf
in the garden," but you haven't heard it howl.

Really, it's not anything at all. Even
the moon's—unfleshed face—is only C sharp,

a trill, in the music you—is it dance to?
I forgive your—unpracticed steps. Forgive mine.

But the wrong notes are still—upchucking behind the curtain.

   3.

Stalls the grammar—like a car broken down
in the surf—resembles you? Frilly, this border,

but broader than your day time. And your night
time? Come to me smelling of morning's ditches

and I'll touch your muddy body, I'll touch
your muddy body with my inside out

semantic gloves. What do you think of the thesis
whereas the subject has lost hope of being

mâitre du silence? Thanks for asking. Let me
call in my scholars: Time's rampant waters—

crepitating champagne sands—pattering atoms.

   4.

The wind feeding on—brightness—is the wind
whipping every leaf of the prism that bushes

in the H2O—devoted to its motion.
Oh what a commotion—have we here. Put

your ear picklock to the murmur—do you hear
the boundaries blipping? Great and altering—

is love. The breakers that harmony salutes
bathe in the wish to be—distributed.

Impasto, this knob of seed—*Will work for
a circular return to origin.*

Seeking assistance of brusque, agitating rain.

5.

Dear Ruskin, you say the Uffizi—is
fussy—where "cloud is cloud and blue is blue"

and never the two shall—fuse. Often so.
But the marble floors are like gravel—greened

by backlit boughs—like the hues you saw Tuesday
as the clouds "melted and mouldered away

in a dust of blue rain." If *abyss* had been
—the thing—then as now—would you have liked it?

I thought you'd strike a handsome pose with your hair
of locally inflected cloud, but even you

ambled—out of the frame—as was your right—not to say

6.

your pleasure—your chains easing off like the big-
chinned Klickitat when it leaves the dock—its wide

mouth slowly shutting—the people's heads ever
tinier—pills, you've seen ant pills were heartier.

But that's you, couldn't stand up for me—couldn't
bother to be—my outline and range—old-style

entelechy. To surface-splash a place
while gulls screech-comb the foul chaos of your hair—

which is not there—not a luxury that is there—
I mention it to explain the difficulty.

You know that geometry's no fire. It *holds*. Shake it

7.

it will not—give you more. It neither seeds nor
foams. When I saw them raw spots on the hen's

scrawny neck I hated the whole fuckin'
tribe. Comes from—being—penned up together.

I'm for the kick-grass chickens—on chicken-
shit-spotted byways. Oh, give me a home

where the clouds piss or pass like Saint Peter
healing the sick with his shadow. There's crib

activity in—*shadow,* dude. "I do not
state leaf. I like to beg very much stream."

Each passing thing's—viaticum. Note the air's dress—

8.

tell me when last you saw her out of fashion.
The body's sourced in a sauce it can't wipe—

off—is still warm, still smells of Cook's secret
blend of space and spices. I threw a stick

into the pond for my dog—he returned
dragging pleats of dawn's silken cellophane.

Good boy, keep the make-believe duck, I'm for
the ripples—pulsed like song's—hand on the throat

vibrations. Sometimes September's like June,
plus a gray—skulking fleet of—submarine

impulses. Ping! I'm not angry, but I have to lie

9.

down. If I had a music I'd give it
to everyone wounded. Six are the wounds:

the eyes—ears—skin—nose—tongue
and the feelings. I would not allow the whole

waste of any scrap, I would say to the cat,
I thought you came out from the shadows with

a pale mouse—in your mouth—but it was a strip
of sunlight instead: ticket—laughter—stanza.

If there's no hurry is there ever *not*
any music? The storm windows' deep-drawn

woodwind. The moth's fitful snare stick on the shade.

10.

The surface of last scattering—uncoupled
from matter—is hardly less together

than we are—given, as we are, to the eye
eating its meals. "I had a Chaffin's Finch

today," smacking its lids. Twenty-three motor
bikes vrooming in the living room are not

more ready to go—than our ungoing nerves.
Or call us the wind's violin—the strings

entangled in our wounds. It's a splintered
threshold that awaits the *tutto*'s footfall—

like a wolf whose fur smells of math and burning woods.

each bound of the fiery paper

1

Who does me this I whistle off
brazen as the green of the Palestinian flag

Strange wishful little books clot my fur
I do not labor except to season my domain

Through seven holes all things twitter
I reject the disjecta of allegory

A sluttery roller skate grips my shoe

2

Is there enough chaos in you to make a world?

The feather on the egg is the horse under the bed

The New England winter is still raw and long

The summer is intense and abandoned

PROPAGATION IN THE FOOT, LEG, ARM, AND TRUNK POSITIONS OF BALLET

You are light wine in a wooden leg.
It's a joy to have you in my face, Suzy Peril—
you're not frightened, are you, dear, or delicate?

: Talk about a broad
with an algebraic festival structure
bedecked with a weather of turbulence,
and I know her. She's all spring-legs,
like your frog prince.
        (And, just between us, she's nibbled his thigh.)

: I've seen you girls in your Mary Jane gardens.
But a snapping torso's a 'gator elegance.
Deal with it.
No apologetic thing's
a pilot in these waters.

: come, let's have a squabble. It's almost as good as sex
that leaves a fluttery thing lying half dead,
                        her black eyes reflecting the sun's
    pink cling-glow, and in her head comes drumming now
        the purple sea of evening,
one orange ship leaving,
                        off to Swansea or La Havre.

: I call this dance "The Fire that Creates
Diversion in the Void," and this one
"Barefoot in the Garden of the Nebula Dahlias."

: I remember now I was Aphrodite
                of the silk, shark, and shattered atoms.
And if you want to hear thought in its whoosh-up hour,
come back tomorrow and put your ear to the boards.

: it's hatred of the institution

74

    of stone and alone
that's the redistribution I'm having

: Yes,
I was *turba,*
just as dirty as it sounds.

Many at the Source

"War is the father and king of everything"
—Heraclitus, 53 DK

When all around you the sea air is the bronze-hammock snore
of a god on a crystal island, I almost believe your talk
of "the illusion of predicates,"
"the neutral heart of the multiple,"
and other Latin ghosts that won't get one laid
in the heaven of what shines and sounds
because it isn't language.

You're too gentle to welcome flare-ups,
but any color's a pig noise, wetted freshly,
remarried to the rude and real—
as you speak I see behind you
the green axes of the water striking water.

Bohr was right to be shy of talking about "reality,"
but I miss in your realm of stateless atoms
something raffish, like your lowest tones,
or why not a moan from far-off sea-sucking clouds?
Why not love?

THE PARTRIDGE IN ME

The partridge in me
  is the sugar of caprices
    the partridge roof
      a clamor of resuscitations

He's so evolved
  his shadow so petite
    under his feather thrilled
      belly his slow particular feet

The assassins shoot at him
  their antidotes to perfection
    but a PUNT with PLUTO
      is to him so sweet
        it's DARK SUGAR
          in his butter-yellow beak

No one has found his
  titanium teeth they think
    they've stuffed him but
      THEY DON'T KNOW NOTHIN
      boors are they
        sans interruption

The partridge is crazy
  but he doesn't mind
    he says Hey really I'm okay
    I doesn't mind

Careful like the stars at night
  he steps through the town
    odorous as mimosas

VA, PENSIERO

Orion with his foot to the pedal; rain
spitting silver light on the window;

the *please repeat the last signal*; the *here
conclude my unfortunate adventures*

—leave us, poor itches, we give you
this advice, leave us, side-stitches, a whole

simmer summer is to lease.
The egrets' white gothic brackets

fail to stall the Arno. In the park, winged
messages practice on Mercury's arms.

Remove your stretcheth-forth-the-heavens robes,
you heavens, swim like a bucket among the berries.

Yes, impedimenti, be gone, for along
the streets stroll the beauties,

flexing their fabulous behinds. We are eager
to plant strawberry mentions on your grave.

Your disruptions are as feckless as the bomb
that busted the Ponte Santa Trinita.

Poor ditches, we have news for you:
they fetched the Primavera's head from the Arno

and put it back on her neck.
The beautiful, broken-nosed thing.

They put it back on her neck.

Mine and Not Mine This Happiness, Sucked up into the Nobody Dark

I take refuge in breath
        (this one,
                (now this one,
refuge in sea-air,
          the senses
slewing into it
             the way one horse
leans into another
   as they run around a pasture;

refuge in the tiny sailboat that stole
out from behind the vase on the sill
                         and bounced away
  breathing the many breaths of the sea,
       as if breath itself were the abode

      (breath of what god,
             chemical, chimerical,
   whose happiness was never meant to be ours?);

     refuge in this breath and this one,
     each both world and sensation,
lest sensation be without world,
     lest world be without sensation.

When a trawler's window-glare
         yoyos down up down
    over the waves at their fold,
       the waves at their fold and tear,

bright worlds scoot and whoop—
          venturing,
   returning—
mimicking breath as if
     to breath belonging.

And now from some fabulous depth of space,
   a flame-papaya moon
        heaves up
   off the rocky point—

      close,
   huge,
           breath's husks igniting.

Why is there any happiness at all?

NUDE SHIVERING AS HE LEAVES THE STUDIO

What's got into me tonight,
    why aren't the credits lost in mist as usual?
    Sara speaking into my ear
like a dozen colonels with blue voices,
    and Peter, describing the way we felt then,
    made a day, there,
       which is here even now,
hidden in ivy like a tennis ball
             orange as a nasturtium.

Come, then, all of you,
       Karen with your ambulance
    attendant's smile,
Skylar with your sobbing laughter, B.J., Nick,
        oh-so-chatupable Joan,
  come now—
      no, *not* brushing the dirt off first,
        but swiftly,
       for I would be
       electric with you,
          with you, pronoun so sweet and burning.

Nothing of the grave will remain in you tonight—
    oh, don't walk with so much cloud in your feet!
      You mustn't burst into tears
          when you see me,
    the unfair one,
          the one who by luck is still breathing.

    For this very night you will be my life.
    There will be
       an insurrection *dans le palais de mort,*
    we will free the microbe guards, we will

clang our goblets under the great wheels of the chandeliers,

Death won't be admitted tonight *dans la chambre de souvenir.*

Acknowledgements

Some of these poems have appeared, usually in somewhat different form, in the following magazines:

Berkeley Poetry Review, BOMB, Boston Review, Catch Up, Canary, Colorado Review, Columbia: a Journal of Literature and Art, Gulf Coast, jubilat, New American Writing, Ploughshares, Poetry International, and *Sonora Review.* Heart-felt thanks to the editors for supporting the poems.

Calvin Bedient was raised in Washington state and received his Ph.D. in English literature at the University of Washington, after studying piano at the Whitman College Conservatory of Music. His first teaching position was at Emory University in Atlanta, Georgia. He then taught at the University of California until his recent retirement. He has been a visiting instructor at Harvard University and the Iowa Writers' Workshop. A founding editor of the *New California Poetry Series*, he now co-edits *Lana Turner: A Journal of Poetry & Opinion*. His reviews have appeared in *The New York Times Book Review, The New Republic, The Nation, Partisan Review, Salmagundi, The Boston Review*, and other journals. His critical books include *Eight Contemporary Poets (Oxford University Press), He Do the Police in Different Voices: The Waste Land and its Protagonist* (University of Chicago Press), and *The Yeats Brothers and Modernism's Love of Motion* (University of Notre Dame Press).
He has published three previous collections of poetry: *Candy Necklace* (Wesleyan University Press), *The Violence of the Morning* (University of Georgia Press), and *Days of Unwilling* (Saturnalia Books). He lives in Santa Monica, California.

The Multiple
by Calvin Bedient

Cover Art by David Goldes
Pouring, 1994
Gelatin Silver Print
© David Goldes, Courtesy of the Artist and Yossi Milo Gallery, New York

Book offset printed by Thomson-Shore, Inc., Dexter, Michigan
on Glatfelter Natures Natural 60# archival quality recycled paper
to the Green Press Initiative standard.

Omnidawn Publishing
Richmond, California
2012
Ken Keegan & Rusty Morrison, Co-Publishers & Senior Editors
Cassandra Smith, Poetry Editor & Book Designer
Gillian Hamel, Poetry Editor & OmniVerse Managing Editor
Sara Mumolo, Poetry Editor & OmniVerse New-Work Editor
Peter Burghardt, Poetry Editor & Bookstore Outreach Manager
Turner Canty, Poetry Editor & Features Writer
Jared Alford, Facebook Editor
Juliana Paslay, Bookstore Outreach & Features Writer
Craig Santos Perez, Media Consultant